LIZZIE BORDEN IN LOVE

Crab Orchard Series in Poetry

Editor's Selection

LIZZIE BORDEN IN LOVE

POEMS IN WOMEN'S VOICES

Julianna Baggott

Crab Orchard Review

&

Southern Illinois University Press

CARBONDALE

16   15   14   13   5   4   3   2

The Crab Orchard Series in Poetry is a joint publishing venture of Southern Illinois
University Press and *Crab Orchard Review*. This series has been made possible by
the generous support of the Office of the President of Southern Illinois University
and the Office of the Vice Chancellor for Academic Affairs and Provost at
Southern Illinois University Carbondale.

Crab Orchard Series in Poetry Editor: Jon Tribble

Library of Congress Cataloging-in-Publication Data

Baggott, Julianna.
Lizzie Borden in love : poems in women's voices / Julianna Baggott.
p. cm. — (Crab Orchard series in poetry)
I. Title. II. Series: Crab Orchard award series in poetry.
PS3552.A339L59 2006
811'.6—dc22
ISBN-13: 978-0-8093-2725-6 (pbk. : alk. paper)
ISBN-10: 0-8093-2725-2 (pbk. : alk. paper)   2006006450

Printed on recycled paper. ♻

The paper used in this publication meets the minimum requirements
of American National Standard for Information Sciences—Permanence of
Paper for Printed Library Materials, ANSI Z39.48-1992. ⊗

This Book Is Dedicated to the Women within It

Contents

Acknowledgments

I'm thankful to the following publications, where poems in this collection first appeared:

Beloit Poetry Journal—"Helen Keller Dying in Her Sleep" and "Marie Laurent Pasteur Watches Louis Walk to the Kennels after His Stroke"

Crab Orchard Review—"Monica Lewinsky Thinks of Bill Clinton While Standing Naked in Front of a Hotel Mirror"

Image—"Dorothy Day's Daughter, Pregnant with Her Ninth Child, Begs Her Mother for Charity: A Bedtime Prayer" and "Ethel Water's Mother, Louise--Raped at Twelve--Cannot Listen to Her Daughter Sing 'His Eye Is on the Sparrow'"

Meridian—"Katharine Hepburn in the Attic with Her Dead Brother"

Quarterly West—"Mary Todd on Her Deathbed"

The Southern Review—"Irene, Suicide, Four Years after Divorcing Norman Rockwell and Marrying Francis Hartley, Jr.," "Mary Rockwell after Her Son Is Accidentally Stabbed While Fencing" and "To Mary Rockwell, now dead"

32 Poems—"Mary Rockwell, 1950" and "Marie Curie Gives Advice to Her Daughter Irene before Her Wedding"

Third Coast—"Ida Saxton McKinley, the First Lady, Seizes during a Dinner Party" and "Mary Cassatt, Going Blind, Crosses Her Room"

TriQuarterly—"Mrs. Dali"

Virginia Quarterly Review—"Camille Claudel Bathing in the Lake near Chateau D'Islette," "Camille Claudel Does Not Want to See the Baby," "Camille Claudel Refuses to Sculpt Clay Given to Her by Sister Saint Hildefonse at the Asylum," and "Lori Schappell, a Conjoined Twin, Addresses the Kmart Cashier Who Eyes Her with Too Much Sympathy"

"Mary Todd on Her Deathbed" was reprinted in *Best American Poetry 2000.*

"Mary Rockwell, 1950" was reprinted in *Red, White, and Blues,* an anthology of poetry from the University of Iowa Press.

LIZZIE BORDEN IN LOVE

Lori Schappell, a Conjoined Twin, Addresses the Kmart
Cashier Who Eyes Her with Too Much Sympathy

You don't know the forest
of two minds bound by weeds
grown from one to the other,
the synapses like bees
        cross-pollinating
our honeyed brain.
When my sister sings,
the bones of my skull are her resonance.

Your mind is a yeast packet,
unbroken, unrisen. Today
how often will you think: *Price Check*
and each time the thought will stall
with lonesomeness.

Yet you think my sister is a bulky hat
stitched to my head.
You, untethered, drift through life.
And we pity
   you and the other self
you hide in your throat.

3

THE ROCKWELL POEMS

Irene, Suicide, Four Years after Divorcing Norman Rockwell and Marrying Francis Hartley, Jr.

Claw-footed, white, enameled iron, the water rises;
    And where is my husband —the brawny aviator,
the Olympic broad-shouldered fool? Most likely,
telling war stories to other oafs —the old broken rudder,
his airplane sinking in the English Channel;
he sent out carrier pigeons and waited for rescue.

      No one is coming for me.
These restless Brookline pigeons —a window of them —
foul the sill.
    My mother is dead now, and I've spent
        too many hours —years —
under the eye of nurses, those asylum hallways —
iron beds clanging walls —
and the insane cry like gulls and buoy bells.

      I'm one of them.
Mrs. Norman Rockwell
      is someone else now, and I'm glad of it.
Hoddy, my sweet brother, lewd, vulgar, pink Hoddy,
he'll deny that I drowned myself in a tub as he denied that I was
a wild girl, who could not be trusted alone with men.
He'll huff and scowl, knowing, even as he says he does not,
that I let the water weight my lungs.

    And the pigeons will continue to rustle
and coo like the ladies of New Rochelle.
      What will they say of me now?
I have already killed myself a thousand times.

Will their husbands —those lolling, docile dogs —
remember me with a desperate ache, a twitch?

Dear *Saturday Evening Post:*
I am blue and cold, legs sprawled, floating head, a woman
    —so middle class, yellow bathroom tiles so cheery —
drowning herself in a white tub.

Mary Rockwell, after the Abortion

Look at me, Norman. I'm smiling at you.
I've been beaming from New Rochelle
to Hollywood, aboard the German cruise ship
and back.
It didn't hurt, surprisingly. Not much,
                    my sweet genius.

I've been thinking today of Peter Levine
 —the poor kidnapped boy who stopped
at the electric shop to buy wire to fix his skates
but never came home, bowlegged
and typical enough
        (to be one of our own);
we left that news story behind us.

And our three boys will not go missing
like Peter (head sawed off, limbs
eaten by fish)
and there will be just three Rockwell boys.
(Let the men in rowboats troll for Peter's head.
Nothing will be found. Here, either.
It is just tissue, the doctor told me, only that!)

Look at our photographs —you wear your guilt,
an awkward formality, hands covering
        the source of this weighty accident,
but I'll distract them.
I'm a woman, laughing, on a family vacation,
a mother,
    a corsage fiercely pinned to her coat.

9

Mary Rockwell, 1950

I exist as water stained with tea.
It is irreversible. I'm only the window pane,
defined by your sun or your clouds.
You never demanded it; did you? (Did you?)

Sometimes they introduce me —Mary, the wife
of Norman Rockwell —but I don't hear wife —
I hear leg. Some have lost them
and lived on quite fine, pinning pants beneath a stump.

I can't remember how it got started;
    Once there was something
to make right and I rejoiced
        because I could right it.

The day after our wedding, driving up
Fifth Avenue, I spotted a man in a top hat.
A top hat! Three more in front of the plaza
climbing out of a Rolls-Royce!

And my heart is now propped falsely
        with exclamation marks.
I should have stolen each canvas
    before you overworked them,

but really, Norman, I am your greatest creation —
drunk, insane, raw.
        Can't you hear the critics,
finally happy?

Now as they gaze at me —
your Pollock, if ever there could be such a thing —
and gaze and gaze, they see a portrait, Mr. Rockwell,
of the real, unbeloved American truth.

Mary Rockwell after Her Son Is Accidentally Stabbed While Fencing

There was no button on the tip?
An accident? Is there such a thing?
But they say you will not die.
I am the one drawn to sharp edges,

to windows and bridges,
to bottled motors pouring fumes,
to the sweet ether of gas. I am confined
to squirrel and nest, to deny

the dark lake's promise of sleep.
Norman paints this world,
scrubbed, secured, coddled,
and someone must keep track

of its underbelly, how death so adores us
it doesn't take my son, *take me* —but lurks.
My job is to return fan mail:
Baltimore, Dayton, Hingham . . .

And to harbor the half-life of grief,
the dark room, the poisoned flask, pills,
the pear folding itself, in a chorus
of flies, back into the earth.

Let me tell you this, son —
in our cardigans, bathrobes, boat shoes
we are all dying of pierced hearts
in the light of this rosy day.

To Mary Rockwell, now dead

They thought you'd finally killed yourself.
                    Well, of course.
You had lived with the threat for so long
it had grown smooth as a stone
                    in their pockets.
You wore suicide —not the whole gown —
but accessories —one day its shoes, another
its hat. You offered it to yourself each day
like a slice of toast, like a lemon tart,
like a walk round the lake on the hottest day
in summer. *A swim?*
Did you get to glimpse the irony —
after all of your staging, this sudden death, unplanned,
as if a banquet can simply break out,
as if a wedding party has appeared on the lawn
with lanterns floating in the limbs of trees
as if
your fourth child, the one aborted by the Brit,
        was born, after all, and grew —
how he loves you, how time turns,
how death swells, tastes
                    nothing like you would expect
and greets you with a rushing lion's love.
Or not. A light switch fails, a bulb gives
a hollow ping; the room is dark.

Mary Todd on Her Deathbed

I can hear them, choking on spoons, screaming
in shower stalls; the fat are given only
a raw egg and whiskey
        and those who refuse to eat
are force-fed. The least crazy sing,
picking scalp scabs in window seats.
One woman finds scissors
        and stabs herself
again and again. It was the tireless Jew
who wore me down; no one believed
that he followed me
        from train to train
with his satchel of poisons, sneering
as they searched my baggage
for the stolen hotel footstools, how he knew
that I shuffled because my petticoats,
stitched so tight with money,
        had become a heavy net
for dredging the lost. And I do not speak of the lost:
Abe could have worn me as a boutonniere,
my pinched face, say it: an ugly plump bud,
hoisted skirts and petticoats
        the leaf and ribbon trim.
I remember the hoisted skirts,
how his body seemed
        a long white country of its own.
But it was owned by a country
of citizens as unruly as my dead boys,
my dead boys
        roaring through the White House.

Nothing was mine, after all. Strangers
crowded his open coffin, snipped souvenirs
from the curtains,
       slipped hands
into the casket to unclip his cufflinks.
All the while, they could hear me
          wailing from bed.
Every day I can move slightly less;
each body hinge becomes more stubborn
         than memory.
I know how I will die: a clenched jaw,
fists gripping bed sheets. Stiff with longing,
I will have to break
       into heaven, the willows
in my handmade girlhood hoop-skirt snapping.

Marie Laurent Pasteur Addresses Louis in Her Mind
While She Scalds the Sheets

Without you, I would know nothing
about what festers —germs,
their heated breeding,
        their love without exhaustion.
What does death look like, Louis,
held by your microscope for inspection?
I know it intimately
            worn on our children's faces —
the scalding of typhoid fever, the wrung mouth,
the loosened eyes. I would recognize it anywhere.
It charmed me that you forgot our wedding,
instead dithering in the laboratory,
bent to your microscope, living among
the unseen.
        But now my sin is a weak desire
for ignorance. I adore the boy at the market
with the cleft in his skull,
            a dent from a shovel.
He believes the world of bushels,
onions and seed,
what can be held in his giant fists
and seen by his wide-set, pitching eyes.

Marie Laurent Pasteur Watches Louis
Walk to the Kennels after His Stroke

Once I wished his brain would remain unhitched,
and the world would go on ignorantly without him.
I asked him questions —
How old are you, Louis?
>   *I'm a boy.*
Aren't you a great man of science?
>   *A great man of science?*
Have you had a lapse, have the doctors come?
>   *The doctors won't come. They're afraid.*
And what are they afraid of?
>   *The others. Hear them?*
Sick with mad-wolf disease,
they scream through the streets.
Are you a little boy living in Arbois?
>   *Yes, of course.*
But dutiful logic returned, good dog with a stick,
and Louis is not crazy or dead, only scarred,
    left hand pinned to his chest.
From the window by the sink
            where I scrub my hands,
I watch him drag his gimp leg
across the yard like a weighty hoe.
His brain, once again, folds and unfolds
like a hand cupped with silkworms,
        oh, the fine threads of thought.
He will light the alcohol lamps,
flame the syringes
        and tend to his rabid dogs.

Mary Cassatt, Going Blind, Crosses Her Room

I bored my eyes into the yellow boat, the blue
armchair,
     into footbaths, lamps, and
stitching, humming women yes,
      their babies, cheeks luminescent
as lit globes,
       and now everything
—even the toreador's smoke, the door's slick knob,
the chamber pot and window seat —
       has eyes
that watch me as I tour this —
      a blind woman's tidy room.
It is like starving to death by a closed throat
and I only recall the tartness of a berry.
I want to eat.
     It's a death before death.
Ladies, I dream of you now,
the orchard, the opera, the omnibus.
I've preserved your quiet lives,
    but who will give shape to mine?
The mind's eyes are horrid; the air isn't paste,
the world —aghast in detail —
      is made of splinters.

Katharine Hepburn in the Attic with
Her Dead Brother

Easter Sunday, the neighbor's lawn tufted
with colored eggs,
      but I won't see them until later, until keening
in the doctor's yard, the girl with the shorn head —
and the dead brother?
      Tom. His face distorted, I would have said
it wasn't him, blue, swollen, bulged, but I knew
      his bare feet. I would have said it wasn't
our attic, but I knew the boxes
              marked *Holiday.*
It begins here, two bodies, both my own.
One is cutting the rope
           with her mother's sewing scissors.
The other is acting like a young girl cutting rope.

THE BEURET-CLAUDEL-RODIN POEMS

Rose Beuret in a Cool Bath While a Servant
Reads the Society Pages to Her

(Rose Beuret was Rodin's long-term, senior mistress, before, during,
and after his relationship with Camille Claudel.)

"Tonight, at the Daudets', the little Claudel,
Rodin's pupil . . .
                    Should I go on Madame?"

Yes. Begin again!

"Tonight at the Daudets', the little Claudel,
Rodin's pupil, wearing a canezou embroidered
with large Japanese flowers, with her childish face . . .
her witty sayings in that heavy country accent."

In Brussels, you know, the air swelled in summer.
Auguste and I swam through it. Swans.
Dirty unknown swans.
      M. Rodin preened me from stone.
I was his sole admirer, the lowly seamstress
whose heart pounded with more grunted, hearty favor
than hordes of Parisiens can muster.
My pin-pricked fingers beaded blood,
                    and once, only once,
I stained a dress at its hem. Cold water, salt.
This I know —how to pull blood from silk.
                    Begin again!

"Tonight, at the Daudets', the little Claudel,
Rodin's pupil . . ."

Oh, our dull witted son. Hear him shuffle
through the dusty house. Hear him bang
a wooden spoon across the railing
like a prisoner, begging for his father —a lesson
I've taught him well.

   We will not be seen at the Daudets'
nor the Goncourts'. Can you hear them saying
Poor Rose Beuret. Poor, poor Rose,
pruning this minute in a tub. Not even a shunned wife,
only an aged mistress.

   Don't look up from the paper.
Stitch your eyes to the page. How I sag, my stomach
as scarred as the helmet maker's wife.
     Continue!

 wearing a canezou embroidered
with large Japanese flowers, with her childish face

Draw the shutters against the sun.
Tomorrow I will hire two more servants.

Have I grown deaf? I cannot hear you.
    Speak up! Speak up!
I want to hear it: Madame Rodin, Madame Rodin!

Yet the name barely sounds out —
  like my drowned fist pounding the tub.

Camille Claudel Bathing in the Lake near Chateau D'Islette

In a few days, a new bathing costume will arrive by post.
Auguste Rodin —I've told the illustrious bull to buy me one
at the Bon Marche.
        Imagine him —dusted white —

wooly and dazed as a big sheep among the hive of women,
 —the flit and dither of motion.

        Hold still, he would tell them.
Turn, turn, lift, yes, there. Don't move.
A glimpse of swollen calf,
        the hand's raised veins.

But the women of the Bon Marche wouldn't listen.
They know better than to believe that life

        is raised up out of stone.
Of course he won't go to the Bon Marche.
He will send one of Rose's servants
with a note: one bathing costume —

dark blue with white piping, two pieces,
blouse and pants (medium size).

He will say it's for one of his models in Azay —
he eases into lies like a woman into a lake,
a brilliant woman into a lake.
(I am convinced of my genius,

and there is no greater lover than my own genius.)
The servant will tell Rose who will fume and cry —

her face, a rose, yes, as a rose is a furious fist.
In the overripe garden, he'll pick at the dry plaster
on his corduroy and worry over my mood
and tell his favorite story to an assistant —

the one about me and the birds in Renoir's house
trapped in the shutters, how I opened the latches

and watched them burst into the sky.
Rodin is jealous (like a mother of a brilliant daughter).
Each time I slip under water
—how easy it is to disappear;

the world filled with thieves —
          the lake's surface is a lit window.

Camille Claudel Does Not
Want to See the Baby

I have been humbled, this hunching
to the piecemeal stitches of a skull
not passing through but rising
from my own seam.
What shocks —the wet moss
of black hair.
I can hear the nursemaid
hushing a mouth that rings out.

    Noise is swept to the corners;
the broom propped by the door.
Night is a dark cherry

    pressed by the throat of Day.
I remind myself that I did not want
to be a mother

    (like my mother),
but how stubborn that small moment
of seeing —the baby, balling up,
knowing the world's keen eye
is upon him —knees springing
to his blotched chest,

    feet folded in prayer.

Camille Claudel in Her Studio in Quai Bourbon

A cleaning lady poured powder into my coffee,
and while I slept,
>   she stole the Woman with a Cross,
and now artists all over Paris only sculpt women and crosses.
Just the same as when M. Picard broke into my house with a passkey.
There stood my Woman in Yellow, and now
he has enough women in yellow to fill an autobus.

This morning I sacrificed four wax models to the fire.

This evening two more must follow.

The windows are padlocked, chained.
All I eat is kept in a packing crate above the window.
But the coals have eyes.
>   Spies pour in through the walls —
they claw.
>   This morning Dr. Michaux's boy
played in the courtyard.
I wandered out in my white dressing gown,
amid my pool of cats, to offer bonbons and advice:
Trust me —there is poison in the salicylate of soda.
Instead for a cure, take infusions of plantain leaves
and burdock roots. Despise M. Rodin, most of all.
If you are found dead in your sleep, I will cry everywhere
that the Protestants poisoned you, and if I die in my sleep,
you must cry the same for me!

And the boy,
cheeks full of chocolates, nodded his head
like Rodin himself, like me,
like a child made from the two of us,
licking his hands like a cat. He cannot be trusted.

Camille Claudel Refuses to Sculpt
Clay Given to Her by Sister Saint Hildefonse
at the Asylum

Hoarding is my only comfort.
It builds,
     and rocks are rocks. It builds and
your brow, Sister, is a brow.

     Your bulbous cheeks
do not stir me. Your dimpled chin means
nothing.
     Keep it to yourself. Your girth.

Your wimple
     and mouth. Your paunch
of chin.
     The small spade of your nose.

Flaunt them —the nostrils tensed
     and fully flowered —
they will not lure my fixed attention.
Recite your Bible:

     The eye cannot say to the hand,
"I have no need of you."
But my eyes tell my hands, *Be still. Hush.*
Don't cry. See how they listen and behave?

If you want me to be sane, I will be
tepid, punctual.
     No clay beneath my nails.
Do all diseases begin as cures?

It must be like the love of God.
Fervor that must be tended —
or the body is a firetrap.
            Forgive me, Sister.

We know each other too well.
Sometimes you walk into my room —
broad and proud as a bridegroom
            and I do not hate you

            and you do not hate me.
Were you a sad child? Did they not love you?
Tell me, my bullfrog.
            Tell me again, my pet.

I will forgive you all of this, my captor.
I will forgive you for this table with its lump of clay.
Slip me a key
and I will speak of you in heaven.

Tomorrow at noon. Let me. Past the gates. Alone.
Think of it —
one of us allowed to leave this place alive!
Watch me, down the blue path.

After a Trip to the Dentist with Sister Saint Hildefonse, Camille Claudel Returns to the Asylum

The car shutters, trees rush past, and children . . .
Imagine, children! They have not all died
from a lack of mother love.
They are not mourned by circling birds.
        No, they bob in schoolyards.
Sister Saint Hildefonse and I left Montdevergues
like white sails, I whispered, *setting out over the Atlantic.*
Together we have had eight teeth pulled,
but pain becomes its own comfort.
Sister Saint Hildefonse is rich bottomed.
Her hands flutter around her bulging cheeks.
In this light —the afternoon sun on her face —
the rocks of this earth desire her shape.
I recall how marble once coveted us all.
Today I do not hate the Protestants, the Huguenots,
the Freemasons; Rodin is a breathy whisper.
Sister Saint Hildefonse prays through her nose
while I cast my starved eyes on the world.
And we are carted through this Avignon,
our mouths tight with clotted cotton,
our heads bundled shut —

        the way we are preferred.

Camille Claudel Dies after Thirty Years
in the Asylum

Dead Mother, I despise you. Is it your punishment
to watch me suffer and die? At night, I open my eyes
and I see your eyes. My jailer. Kiss me on the mouth.
Taste this death, Widow Claudel.
        Will you miss this spectacle:
the chipped chamber pot, the oily black sauce
of soured beef stew, tough figs and biscuits?
Will you miss the iron bed? Or Sister Saint Hildefonse,
no saint, herself afflicted a bit, tender with her own
wretchedness, teary with nerves?

        I will limp to you
with the sort of packages you sent to me these years:
one kilo of butter,
one kilo of flour,
one piece of soap.

(The lunatics are singing like angels of death.)

Beg me, Dead Mother, for mandarins,
for brandied cherries. Beg me for release.

For Sylvia: Come Winter. Come, Winter.

I would give you back to yourself
                if I could —
here, before you knew much —
Sylvia Plath, Fulbright scholar modeling
the latest fashion: a white swimsuit
with black polka dots, high heels,
long legs
as stiff and posed as two young soldiers.
I thought of you this morning,
the oven, the lush unceasing offers
                of death.
And how I long, today,
to stall in the yard, the mail flipping
in my hands while the house parts
a field of wind.
Look! Leaves build at the door.
Here, in the dirt, bulbs.
        The crocuses keep patient time —
        those blind eyes, buried —
but the sun will cause
                an inner ticking
that only the bulbs can hear
dim as a fragile pulse in the ear.

Minna Edison Listens to Her Husband Give
a Lecture around the Time He Is Deciding to Disown
Thomas Edison, Jr., Minna's Stepson

How many volts to kill a Coney Island elephant?
I have no knowledge.
                    But this —your son so lost
because of a chorus girl, a lush —
I know you should not turn away from him.
Motherless, he was a little in love with me —
(A young second wife is apple-sweet!)
or were you too busy in your laboratory
to notice his love letters, his boundless
pawing affection, his unearthly need?
The companies who use his name for their
Wizard Ink Pills, their Magno-Electric Vitalizer,
claim cures for bone aches, for blindness,
but not this,
          the despair of stark disappointment.
Oh, how a name can weigh and darken!
And sons cannot be invented from tungsten.
Please, Wizard of Menlo Park, don't tell us again
how the motion picture stutters to life,
                    don't tell us how
the phonograph whirs, then purrs, then sings.

Margaret Sanger Addresses the Ghost
of Ida Craddock

Ida, is it you? Gauzy as a bride, at long last.
Do you instruct the virgins of heaven
               with pamphlets?
Sit here, on the edge of my bed.
             Oh, Ida,
Comstock is dead
          —is that why I see you now? —
the angry man full of piss, fat on the fat
of his wrongheadedness,
         his brain a pink lard ham.
Why did you breathe poison for him?
         When I feel bereft, I think of you
and girls on wedding nights,
white gowns damp with blood
      —and I am often bereft these days;
     my daughter is dead, pneumonia.
             Women,
sometimes we cannot breathe. I'm tired.
    I admit I've imagined Comstock in the tub,
his cheeks flushed in shame,
             his defiant cock
grotesquely swollen, a naughty soldier,
his own criminal
       in a meaty cap.
You'll be happy to know he caught cold
at my husband's trial, then died.
         A certain justice.
And I hope they plant old Comstock
beneath the Virgin Mary —

you were no virgin, Ida, so be it, and, for me,
there will be many, a promise,
　　my William, my Havelock, lovers.
I take as many as I want.
　　Why did you let yourself slip away?
　　　　Revive me.
Comstock is dead, but there are women dying everywhere.
　　Ida, tell me again how much we cannot speak of.
　　　　Oh, these Gods and Masters!
Will roots sift through his coffin
　　　　and find Comstock's shrunken soul,
a useless gland in him, a goldfish, flipping, breathless
　　　　if not long dead?
And there on his grave, season after season,
I hope the lewd flowers rise,
　　　　a riotous orgy of fornication —
the earth ashamed to embrace our enemy after all;
Imagine, Ida, gladiolus, birds of paradise, rearing
　　　　an abundant perverse blush.

Monica Lewinsky Thinks of Bill Clinton
While Standing Naked in Front of
a Hotel Mirror

We will watch each other age
in front of cameras, in newsprint,

a public decay. It's already started.
Look at my new sway;

my body seems more ample
among the miniature shampoos,

the thin rectangles of wrapped soaps.
Look at the pale shifting of my skin

under the red eye of the ticking heat lamp.
And I've noticed your hair's gone white,

your face loosening.
                    I'm shocked

how you can still appear —
not televised, not some public memory

of the two of us swimming valiantly —
but the intimacy of teeth,

            breath and breathing.
And I carry you sometimes

            for a day or two,
like a bird hidden in a pocket

        and I imagine
that you know how I live.

        And while the bird shifts
and rustles and keeps one wet eye

on my life, I am more purposeful.
I stride.

        But today you see me here, naked,
standing in front of this hotel mirror.

You are someone who knew me before
I was the world's collective joke

about cigars, thongs, stained dresses,
when I was a girl named Monica.

I miss her much more than I miss you.

Mrs. Dali

Let me explain: Salvador remembered
medical books opened
like a woman's legs, his father's fat finger
pressed to flatten pages —*Look*, the old doctor said,
this is how you can go crazy, my son,
sores, lesions, puffed and seeping.
I wasn't raised with such fears. I loved men
like so many rows of chocolates and my husband
did not deny me my weakness. He understood
weakness. *Hush. Isn't fear a weakness?*
I wonder if you've imagined it, the surrealist's sex?
Do you think that he fashioned his erect penis
to resemble the blurred face of Lincoln,
or timed his climax with an umbrella pop,
and there, rising, a man hung by his neck.
This was enough: we locked till our souls mingled.
His moustache was not winged, but waxed stiff.
The two of us, our desperate aging flesh —
the realism became unbearable, absurd.

THE BORDEN POEMS

Lizzie Borden Addresses Her Jury of Men

I needed the prussic acid for my sealskin cape;
it was infested.
        Arsenic in the mutton?
There were no signs of poison;
I could hear the hymns of flies
as those two bodies —airing naked, butchered —
awaited autopsy
        on the dining-room table.
(Oh, how she became the fatty beef
placed at the spot for her own platter!)
Their two stomachs, knotted and sent off,
        were found pure.
I was my father's favorite; he always wore
the pinky ring I gave him, quite like
        a wedding band
in that it bound us. He understood the tether.
And she was not my mother —
Abby Durfee Gray, his scowling wife —
her father was only a tin-peddler
        with a pushcart of sundries,
and she was once an old sallow maid,
        (like my dear sister Emma).
He saved that ancient whale from the dust of aging
alone among trinkets —
    but who would save Emma and me?
No, I needed no saving.
A woman of wealth, of travel (I've seen Lilly Langtry
on the stages of Europe!),
        I was a volunteer
in the Ladies' Fruit and Flower Mission.

During the murders?
I'd been in the barn, as I've stated,
searching for metal to fashion sinkers
for a fishing trip to come.
      The barn floor was covered in a layer of dust?
My footprints were not there?
        Let me explain, dear sirs.
Look again into my pale, damp face,
so like your daughters', sisters', wives'.
We ladies only know what we are taught.
We are your creations:
      porcelain hands, hearts sublime.
We are not real —that's why
there were no footprints in the dust: We float.
And my father made me. You all recall
      my father, the richest man in town:
as a young entrepreneur
his caskets were the first to come with
        a money-back guarantee,
and, yes, I've heard the rumors
      that he cut off the feet of his dead clients
to fit them into smaller, cheaper coffins
  —and, for that, did he use an axe?

Lizzie Borden in Love

Leave the hired palm trees, the orchestra,
    the blazing gaslight chandeliers —
(the Borden's house is on the Hill,
        finally, rightfully,
lit and singing. What would father think
        and his fat wife?
The good Reverend Jubb and the ladies
of Central Congregational, do they hear
           violins?)
       My bedchamber
has a ceiling of gold leaf. Come with me,
Nance, starlet, and undress.
Lizzie Borden, the murderess, is in love.
Let the biddies swarm and buzz.
        I no longer care.
Once I kept love secret, two girls, quiet
attic lovers.
I thought of her when I ate my father's pears.
Rush, hurry.
       My sister, Emma, haunts
the second floor, sugar cubes tucked in
her cheek pockets. Priggish, hateful, dour,
she is praying for our souls,
    and I've come to believe
that God grants her wishes,
      no matter how dark. (Do you recall
the young Boston reporter who printed lies
then slipped under the wheels of a train?)
Our wondrous sinning will not last.

Hurry before Emma

of the black dresses, Emma of the bleak mourning
and rotting teeth,

fixes her end to it. You think I'm strong enough
to wield an axe? Who hasn't looked

at the bulk of my arms and not thought it?
But Emma, hushed Emma, shadowed,

studying birds from her window quite like
a starved cat.

Temperate Emma, Puritan,
she knows how souls turn on family
in the name of love and will never abide this.

How could you understand
what we two sisters have hissed

into each other's ears?
(And, come winter, won't you be gone
and my heart tender and swollen
as an old foot sick with gout?)
The corset of secrets is airless;
Emma and I know love

better than any lovers.

The Night Lizzie Borden Dies

I. EMMA

Patience. Listen.
        Hush my heart.
They've come for me.
      Father? Mrs. Borden?
Dr. Bowen will say it's my mind —gone,
but I know truths; I see shadows more clearly
through this clouded eye.
It's warm. June, but August is a fire
that forever burns inside my chest.
             No one knows heat
the way that I do. Not even Lizzie.
No.
      And now, a pop, in a beam?
I think not. Why am I so bent on living?
It's all I know, this grinding heart.
      The closet is a fake. It hides
a set of steps. If my gristled joints
will hold, there is a wall switch at the bottom
to flood the downstairs with light
      and, just as I like it,
          a hatchet on the wall.
This is what I know of my family:
The one who reaches it first
      will know just what to do.

I am a ghost lifting from my bed to circle.
It is a gift, my gall bladder gone fallow,
    my heart unstitching at last.
It was threaded too tightly, and I have picked
at this one errant loop in hopes of such an end.
From this ceiling height, I can see the rumpy
nurses —this one, here, unloved. It's plain.
I have an eye for that.
Outside, the night is warm,
the stars dizzy,
and Emma, of course, she is the first I will haunt —
though the list is long.
Emma, frantic Emma, oh, sister,
oh, little childless mother,
    I haven't seen this wizened face in years.
I could cup it in my hands.
She runs from me, slips through rooms, and
look how her foot hovers on the stairs
        before it catches.
    Now, hip shattered, she curls
beneath a hatchet.
    I listen to her heated whimper
and if I close my eyes,
it sounds nearly like a woman
        making the urgent noises of love.

The Lion Tamer's Wife after the
Lion's Escape from the Motordome

(Wildwood, New Jersey, 1938)

How do I tell the police that
the lion was my would-be lover,

    that the summer heat sang to us,
and cool October rushed in, an emptiness,

and he was no longer my pet
sitting in the motorcycle's sidecar,

the engine whining as we climbed
the Motordome's steep sides?

I caught him
    watching me with his lion eyes

as I clipped my costume on a line
behind the Casino Arcade.

When did he become a lion again —
    his giant teeth

yawning up into the air of his mouth,
his hair coming forth in redemption?

Do I confess
    I saw the lion drag Mr. Saito's body

beneath the boardwalk, that I can smell
the auctioneer's rusty blood from here?

The auctioneer was a jawing gull —
        I'd have killed him myself.

Can I confess my jealousy?
The lion told me that I am

a harrowed scent, a dart
        of nervous gesture.

He asked me why I belong to Mr. Dobish,
to the motorcycle, to the costume —

        why I belong to the table
where I chew my food —why I belong to the chair.

Even now he would say, Poor, sad Mrs. Dobish
with her bawling husband.

But he isn't here. He's pawing the dead hawker's bow tie.
Does he know that the patrolmen will shoot him

with their service revolvers
and stuff his body as a window display?

And what of me? Mrs. Dobish, fat on longing,
a woman who drives in circles

and dreams of driving in circles —
only her chewed heart is roaring.

Dorothy Day's Daughter, Pregnant with Her Ninth Child, Begs Her Mother for Charity: A Bedtime Prayer

Come to me, Mother, Saint, the basement here
fills with rain and this baby is more tightly lodged
than the last
     for I'm hungry, my ribs draw in
like purse strings
       while this house gives itself back
to the earth and the roof says, *No more.*
It caves, sighing down on us
          in our stiff damp beds.
But I am not a nation, not
     a sickly city that fevers, sweats, cries
for you.
        Go ahead. Tend to *them!*
Bowls, lined up. Soup. Bread.
        As a little girl,
I hated the smitten poor who followed you,
hauling their sun-boiled faces and stench.
     But see how you have forced me
to become one? How else to be loved by you?
     Oh, mother in black. Oh, mother
love. Listen. I am crying now.
The children cry. My husband wades, hauling
water from the basement, and cries.
The torn fields cry. The sun is rasping.
     There is a moment, remember,
there is a time
       when the taut breast gives
and the milk no longer trickles

but charges
      to fill the mouth.
Can you remember
      when you were the breast
and I was the mouth?

Marie Curie Gives Advice to Her Daughter
Irene before Her Wedding

I remember this moment —the pram distilled;
its sediment was an infant,
no longer something born from me,
not residue, not pitchblende,
        but its own particle,
an open mouth, a cry,
within its head, a mind wresting with thoughts
 —my motherland could be there,
driven into the skull,
        some ancient homing.
And now years have passed and I have soaked
in radium.
        I've begun to bleed light.
I hear myself tell you:
A white wedding gown will stain.
Instead choose a navy blue suit
with solid stitching.
        Who says such things?
A woman who despises her own grief;
your father crossing streets in rain —
I see him; the doors are locked,
his umbrella fills with wind,
        the horses approach,
hauling a wagon of soldiers' uniforms —
something to dress the dead —
        it's come to crush him.
And since then I've begun to confuse
        the glowing test tubes

with wicks of the moon, a dazing field of stars,
my own soul, and a moment goes by
when I forget the brutish charm of work.
My hope, daughter, is that
　　what you love doesn't come to kill you,
eye by eye, ear by ear, bone by radiant bone.

The Mule-Faced Woman, 1926

Curtains drawn, I eat peanuts from a paper sack
and read my leather-bound edition
     The Second Book of Wonders,
chronicling the inner workings of a clock.

It is my refinement that shocks.
My elegant legs, ankle-crossed, the shiny twist
of hair, pinned
     by the tattooed lady just so this morning.

Outside, a hammer, a high bell,
the chirp of hawkers, *lookee-here, lookee-here.*
I'm in love with the one who taps the glass
of an eight-legged calf.

     But no one speaks to me.
Each attempt, they converse instead
with my wide nostrils, my eyes set nearly on the sides
of my oversized head so that I must regard them askew,

only when forced to,
     and my jaw, yes, thick as a mule's.
My mother was dainty. She knew that restless heads
envisioned her locked to a horse.

And I was sent off to live beneath a banner,
Mule-Faced, though mules cannot seed.
I wear my burden. My suffering is known.
But, you, seated in the folding chairs —

fat, harrumphing sisters, scolded children
wrenched round by one arm, women
from the hosiery mill dye vats, old ladies
collapsed in prayer, miners, ministers,

oh, all of you in your hats, your frills, your hands
pressed to your hearts,
                    muffling your seized breath,
you may gawk, stare. But I cannot bear

what I see from this little stage.
                              Forgive me
—this world and all of its calamities,
the endless parade.

Ethel Waters' Mother, Louise —Raped at Twelve —
Cannot Listen to Her Daughter Sing
'His Eye Is on the Sparrow'

Lord, I know that the hem of Your robe
could fill a temple —a flood of ribbon,
and now Your hem pours from her mouth?
It is You, Lord, called up from her,
            a song to teach me a lesson
for not raising my own girl.
I would rather listen to barking dogs,
the gagged utterances of the mute,
my own mother crying
            over dirt, a grave.
It is my sadness that Ethel sings, Lord,
my grief riding Your hem.
(This hem will not cure me.)
She may think it is her own sorrow,
but each note, so whole, so unbroken —
so lush it is from Your robe, born
of Your hem that could fill a temple,
that once filled me
(temples can be destroyed)
            and that hem
has always been made of song,
the kind too tender for the world,
the kind only a little pregnant raped girl
can call back into her mouth
and swallow,
      and Ethel was the baby inside
who, there, within my slender ribs —a cage —
first pursed her lips learning
            to suckle and sing my grief.

Ida Saxton McKinley, the First Lady,
Seizes during a Dinner Party

It begins, Love, as a high cough,
the chirrup of a spoon scraping
toward an end, and this tureen —
be calm now, hear me whisper? —
this tureen.
       Mad fit of the body.
(Do not love the invalid. Only love
the girl behind the bank's grillwork.)
Epilepsy is not only stored grief released
       violently into the air.
It is a secret pleasure.
What do you have?
     An office of papers,
the grate of train brakes,
     worry collecting worry —
a decision to preserve yourself
like a berry jam.
You, like this tureen, so calm,
     know nothing of agony,
stitch after stitch —slippers
       for children long dead.
The newspapers will call it a fainting spell —
     How delicate! How ladylike!
But this rugged habit is fit for cowboys.
(Do not look at me with your round eyes.)
Electric, one doctor said.
     (Am I now a modern contrivance?)
Maybe it is that some light snaps on,
my skin begins to burn —the body a lamp

(you used to make my body burn)
and my blood pumps until my neck is fat with it.
My vision goes rigid and I see
     your white handkerchief sailing
toward my face.
(It is not love for me —woman
with clipped hair.)
I know that I am the president's wife —
pitiable with my clipped hair —
but then the comfort comes,
and I am swallowed —lifted, yes, happily,
from your hovered love —
into the shivering throat of a loon.

Helen Keller Dying in Her Sleep

"Suddenly I felt a misty consciousness as of something forgotten,
a thrill of returning thought, and somehow the mystery of language
was revealed to me." —Helen Keller

Here is the pump again, its cool neck,
the well house draped in honeysuckle.
This is before the vaudeville rendition of my miracle,
before the newspapermen took photographs of me
petting the dog, reading Shakespeare,
before I met President Cleveland.
My parents haven't yet talked to Alexander Graham Bell
about my ragged fate.
   I am walking backward,
reaching into my own mouth
for the world's dark syllables.
Anne has returned to me, forever spelling water.
But there isn't a word in my hand
   only a hand in my hand, turning.
It is a mist again, but this time of unknowing.
The returning thought is thought leaving,
escaping, pumped eagerly from my body.
Brain fever, I recall it now,
   my supple mind afire.
Rain water fills a bucket mother left out in the yard.
The doctor is made of rough hands and camphor.
And now it smells like night.